Circumstance
by Harrison Gross

Circumstance.
Alpha edition.
Copyright 2016 Sphirah.
Printed by Amazon.
Front cover, "At the Roulette Table in Monte Carlo,"
Edvard Munch, 1892.
DO NOT DUPLICATE.
ISBN-13: 978-0692682371 (Custom)
ISBN-10: 0692682376

For more information, visit Sphirah.com.

Sphirah is a progressive imprint. Many of our materials are freely distributed on the cloud at Sphirah.com, and our books are printed only to order. This reduces our impact on the environment, maximizes the proliferation of our artists, and keeps our works at a low cost. Our non-exclusive licensing agreements allow our artists to pursue distribution methods as they please. Sphirah was created by the writer, for the writer. Our only ambition is to spread the written word far and wide.

Warm Wishes,

Harrison Reed Gross
Founder & First Chair Poet

For those in hard times, and those in the heights.

A selection of sixty poems in two acts, and a lyrical drama in one...

...for the reader's pleasure.

Act I
Baleful Circumstances

The Spiral

On the occasion of America's tarnishing image abroad,
Winter 2016.

This was a land of grain and iron,
A land of hope and holy fire.
A place where a man's back was enough,
We were a race that never quit in the rough.

This was a country of honest grit,
It prized muscle and honored wit.

What soiled our ivory shores,
What has oiled our glistening seas?
Why does the stench of decay
creep in around me?

It was never a full moon,
There were always slaves.
There were countless caretakers,
and endless unmarked graves.

Yet there was nothing to take but a righteous way,
There was nothing to gain but an honest wage.
Dawn always broke on a shining new day,
We were led by divine sunrays.

Please, let us dispense with all pleasantry.
America in its infancy, now that was a country.
Not this field of shadows,
Not this waste of sorrows.
Not these weathered gallows,
Where just for bread, one borrows.

Where is our freedom,
Our once-golden season?
Can we tear it from the pockets of demons?

It is a foolish thing to think
a man will not answer for his actions.
It was a damning thing to do,
To sunder America into factions.

Tallow House

A garden of magic,
A house of lore.
Step across the humming threshold,
Pass through the vanishing door.

Slide down the slick staircase,
Lift up the hinged floor.
Feel your mind slacken, then race
In the mirrored corridor.

Flicker into the kitchen,
Sample grapes waxen.
A slice of foam toast,
And a cardboard cup of joe.

The paintings follow you,
The statues are all hollow truth.
Every step, a beguiling waver,
With every move you meet your Maker.

Mysterious notes, ghostly and sallow,
Rise out of my rosewood zither.
We come to Tallow
to drink down our silver.

Dreams of Monte Carlo

Rosy faces,
Fine felt,
A beginning—
A hand sets a ball on a wheel.

The Sun, the first play,
The moon ethereal
on the count, the rig,
the steal.

Sinking in the material,
Finding balance in the surreal.
Laying the brick
of a dream palatial.

Patching the keel
of this insatiable vessel,
Mowing down
that nettling thistle.

Doused

Jar of smoke,
Fridge of worms.
Life without you
Is nonstop heartburn.

The snapping moat,
The sparking tightrope,
The flickering out of my only hope.

A sodden oak,
My raspy croak,
In white flames soaked.

Synaptic Coves

Coalition of visages,
Rending traumas.
Viper in burgeoning verdigris.

Burning words
into listing traces.

Where on my star-crossed path,
Where in my lustrous, loamy land,
Is my darling silky hand?

Fire spreads across quicksand.
Greatness is within our grasp,
A clash with the lunging asp.

Boundaries

The poet in faded violet
Slinks 'round brownstones,
Leans on glowing razor wire
Drowning out torn groans.

I am fire, I am alive,
I have risen from my dream dive.
I am seeing things clearly,
I think for the first time.

You are tearing down the block toward me,
You are casting off the scaffold.
You are the embryo of an inferno,
You are a torrential slipstream.

Hot mamba, wreath then constrict,
Stone fox rattling back my last trick.
Misted with monarchs, purest enchantress,
and me a howling dog in the distance.

A shot at happiness,
Perhaps all you will get,
If you're lucky
enough under duress.

Speaking to what
I can say nothing for.
I hear the rap of stilettos,
I hold the lift door.

Park Avenue

These are the fires at eventide,
The brume dividing lives.

This is the bridge
from rag to rich.

This is a venetian blind,
Wool torn from dewy eye.

They toast ancient brandy-wine,
On plush carpets of deepest red dye.

They laugh and prance and cry,
While we sweat, and pant, and fry.

There is no commerce here,
No one has seen a dollar in twenty years.

An owner looses a juicy round
to his howling bloodhound.

It's all on credit, dandy & fine,
My sweet, simple concubine.

There are no workweeks,
You cannot hear the tick of time.

There is no considering
of your truths, let alone mine.

Black Deusenberg ploughing

through crowds of the poor.

These are the eves by fireside,
I am spliced by penthouse door.

There is only a cardhouse of corruption,
Waltzing a hairbreadth junction.

The Foundry

Come, you huddled and ill-conceived patron,
Sample some fare while we hold you for ransom.

This place was supposedly worth a mention,
Yet sourly short of your lofty expectation.

What the hell do you want with us,
As your chef whips up a beef au jus?

Why do you protest and torment,
Stamp out your Sherman and bitterly resent?

I am losing it with these city slicks,
Why go to a bar that costs a brick?

Why do you complain when you can snap,
And build a *Moon Under Water* just like that?

Oh well, enjoy griping
and forking over the bread,
For something your do-nothing wife
could've thrown together instead.

Out of Touch

Swanky pub up the avenue.
Do you have any Hebrew in you?

A humbling beginning to the evening.
This must be the meaning
of biding and preening.

Like a nova-hot poker,
Like me in the deep smoker,
You give me mini heart attacks
Whenever I think of you.

It is self-immolation
to dream of your milky embrace.

Heirs & Luthiers

When the first droll notes
Of joke quartets
Slide around my mind,

Like ribbons lassoing
Tender daydreams
In due measures of time,

Aureate bowstring panoramas
Twinkle and glimmer
With a knowing light.

Yet this colossal rift
Splits the land,
Salts fields once fertile.

Everything tastes like paper
Since I was forsaken
To jagged alleys of peril.

How to hatchet this haze,
How to make a poor man smile
Out of the vile miser's daze?

Break left,
I feel like Flash today.

Auroras rake
Then shimmy away.

Nothing will coil

That rat bastard.

Wealth is a wreath
Of licking flammard.

A Fable Went the Rounds

As American as lemonade,
Cherry as concordant territory.

We are inner tubes
in the lazy river of existence.

From bayou shack to quartz manor,
Will I ever lay my eyes
upon a mane of equivalent splendor?

Canine sweater initiatives,
We are enrobing the nude.
She bought a six-thousand-dollar wedding gown
for her sweet baby bloodhound.

Meanwhile, your American prime
sinks to living above the daily grind.

A stolen story,
A grafted tune,
A cribbed line,
A snatched rune.

The man of
Poe still wishes
For Brigitte Bardot.

Voice of Heaven

It shouldn't be legal to be this thirsty.
Oh right, it's not.

I fought the slaw,
The slaw won.

Foxier than ever,
Stunning as ever.

Dance our Serious Dance.
I get angry,
I get dangerous.

Thinker,
Guerrilla.

Rippling with fury,
Vision growing blurry.

Teardrop explodes,
Soft boys' moonlight.

Infusions of power
and righteousness.

A great tune to lose your mind to.

An echo through airwave,
Chords of ghostly corsairs.

Waterfalling hammers,

See the oil glisten on a pyro.

Hornet burn.
Caring for your Harrison:
I have a high discomfort threshold,
But I prefer low-stress environments.

Toeing the line between
Yorkville peerage and East River bum.

I'm missing my passport,
My clones of Flaubert,
My chameleon charger.

Smoking bandit and hooded menace.
I am tired but not horrible.

Faded, paid in spades,
Wit dripping like a freshly-whet charade.

The One is to give me the one.
Pressures attempt to equalize,
Wading through rubbish and blades.

Temperature

Heat rising,
Then subsiding.
All my fears are colliding.

The rusty gears are grinding,
The calm season never arising.

How to raze
The burning snakes,

How to dream beholden
When you are but a snowflake?

Rustle the hand
I've been dealt.

When you're righteous,
Brilliant as bullion,
Every knot you tie
Is a tight one.

Spirit & Frame

Bag of tricks,
Blustery masticators,
Imposter Phileas Fogg.

Life experience,
Swift wolves.

America's vision,
Sacred mission.

I overstay welcomes—
Jammed back into recognizance.

Assault forms,
Mulch moat.
Thrushes in my beard.

Curtain close.
Boat, dock and port.
Don't care for that sort.

Cubicle Haiku

I wish you were well.
I'm eating cauliflower,
It is unpleasant.

Member of the board
Making vital decision.
It's all for the yacht.

These dreams in clinic,
Defer days of poetry,
But I'm no cynic.

Reproachful, baleful,
Coordinated demise.
Doesn't run, but flies.

Blooming willow beam,
Through center of office drear.
Nature in relief.

Brewing hemlock beer,
Now servicing the account.
Unlocked your dumbphone.

Severest cold front,
Nothing to turn you back now.
Break the silk ribbon.

Rending lava tide.
Your decisions led you here.
Cooling falls of pearl.

Swaying Gait

My chainsaw-juggling, chameleon-frocked friend
might have something to say about that.

What's the rush?
Peace sign,
Eyebrows. Just think,
A man's as good as his wink.

It was a sign to evade that road,
The path of surrendered control.

Bob Dylan had to prove
He was Bob Dylan
To a bunch of boardwalk nothings.

Eyes that differ,
Ears that hear asunder.
Carry death in your pocket,
But spare no blunder.

Maybe, just maybe,
I'll stay here awhile.

Passepartout to my Fogg,
Highly resistant to sin.
I have a hard crust of indulgences.

Triplicate Identity

I

A man is a finely tuned machine.
He is oak of the wood,
See his leaves gleam.

Woman is a warm surround,
Plush as the sunrise
On a dovedown gown.

Needling for someone to step up,
Mime past this action
to the real deal,
the main attraction.

Statuesque,
Carved out of glossy rock.

You are a comic strip,
Bursting with flavor.

Disasters are piling up fast.
Wish you'd step through my looking-glass.

II

Tapestry of a million fantasies,
Sweet mountains.

Scimitar,

Coffers.
Infernal contract.

Brighten your life.
There ain't enough whisky in the world
for how long I've had to live without you.

Whiteness of teeth,
Blackness of blood.

A gent never reverses his word.
Never regrets his decision.

A gentleman walks with a sure step,
Eye on the road,
Hat in check.

She of coconuts,
He of clean linen.
The character satisfies
the urge to be the person.

III

Visual pollution,
Noisy radioactive personage.
Ash your e-cig.

Wondering if I'm on fire.
I am on fire, damn it!

Sinking like wax statue,

SIZZLE sizzle pop

The Jewish is in you,
Cock-a-doodle-doo.

Smashing gear capital,
Sound safe.

Peace, hello, smile.
Nod, tip o' the hat.

See something you like?
Take a picture.

Hat on the tip.
What's shakin'?
Hi there.

Kissing mezuzahs.
Exotic, I like your style.

I'm a squashbuckler,
Entrepreneur extraordinaire.
"You've got to believe."

Thousand-year Cognac

Take a look at this,
My friend of so many years.
This bottle is from our arrears.

Taste the savor of success.
Appreciate what we own,
Every moment is blessed.

Perhaps we will grow
Old as this draught.
Maybe our age will never pass.

The Art of Hospitality

I've really gotten to know
What it means to be at home.
I put on the kettle,
Pick my teeth with bone.

I think I understand satisfaction,
It's never walking alone.
I chop parsley, grind bouillon,
Set some cedar in the stove.

But the butter is melted,
The toast is stale.
This old tea tastes like the mail.

I am withering away,
But for the day I pull back your veil.

Psychedelic Ateliers

Please text me before you undress me.
Please, a flourish when you address me.
You don't have what it takes,
You'll never be my bestie.

This is starting to sound
Like a cheap rap track.
My honey was here,
Then she turned her back.

The needle of goodbye,
I'm not high enough
To speak the truth.

The ash is overflowing,
Scarlet love faded blue.

Is this better
than the old ramshackle flat?
Come on, how can you even ask that?

The crickets are chirping,
The dreams are whirling.
The wax is spinning,
The night is unfurling.

I'm hot as the coil
Of the one working burner.
Bringing soup to a boil,
Wondering if I earned her.

Secret Studio

Dream the sweetest scene,
Make believe you're eating ice cream.

Stride down Park
with demeanor green as grass.

Mischievous mechanics tapping spanners
On frosted glass—
We are surging off the track,
We are never turning back.
Slip into the velvet glamers,
Sigh, recline and relax.

Park Avenue Revisited

How many engines fire in your name?
How many caps tipped before your grace?
How many eyes rise to your tower,
How many clocks tick to your hour?
Is your marble garden weathered smooth?
Is your winter in the warm drawing-room?
Is your blood crisp as Orion in heaven,
Do they sport corsage of golden venom?
Is your worth sworn in vaults on paper?
Your Rolls have the right cylinder?
Do you free the captive with a scrip of waiver?
Do you ride down Park Avenue,
Owed a million favors?

Jackson, Old and Fierce

Talking about that Southern drawl,
Showing the way things tend to fall.

From the mouth of the Missouri,
To White House walls,
He stood proud and tall.

His eyes drank the flurry,
In wake of his footfall.

His vision was never blurry,
He paved our way in a hurry.

Jackson on white horseback,
Heading the army in attack.

With ardor dark ruby,
And bronze statue intact,
He would never lead from aback.

From the coral of our peers,
To the mouth of the Missouri,
He's Jackson, Old and Fierce,
Salute his cold fury.

Down in the Bayou

It was down in the bayou,
Warm ghouls, dusky dew.
Quickly now I saw through
The vixen's lax virtue.

It was on a tore-up Goldwing,
She strummed all my heartstrings.
I sold my liquid things,
and bought a pretty ruby ring.

I told you the fact
In back the liquor shack.
When you go down the bayou,
You ain't never coming back.

It was in the wood, dark like ink,
I felt my soul slip and sink.
Quicksand gone and take me below,
How dark is Dixie on your own!

Swamp did its best to do me in,
My wolves howling with the scent of sin.
All my sorrow, running so thin.
Might drown in the creek with a grin.

Rounding Cape Wrath

I

Am I officially bugging out?
Am I being eaten by my doubt?

Where will my slots set,
What'll be the hand dealt?
Where will the marble rest
On this wheel of fortune's felt?

Where does our future lie,
In ash or in velvet?
It's all on this cast of die,
And naught can help it.

II

I've made bets that would make you quiver,
I have lived in days of danger.

I have downed a toxic draught,
I have smoked tainted reeds.
I am sinking in the past,
I am bound by an iron lead.

All my gold has tarnished,
All my dreams have perished.
When will my curse
be forever banished?

III

When will this dearth
quench and replenish?

It is so cold and dark
When I am without you.

There is no cure for this searing heart,
The night freezes into bitter blue.

IV

Each moment pulses
and you haven't a clue
what passion can be—
I pick the fruit of forbidden tree.

In the mood of the weather,
In the sending of the hand,
I sail a cloudy route
To a sacred land.

V

You can catch me on the horn
any old time.

Tell me that you love me,
over transatlantic

telegraph line.

Clutch close
in arbors of amethyst.

Breath the bliss
of companionship.

Let us turn to art
worth our stewardship.

Let us focus on the Lord
worth our worship.

Cape Wrath bested,
And we slip into the next portent.

Self-portrait Eating an Orange

A swan in rivers of porridge,
The poet out for a forage.
No quarter, but steel courage,
I surge forth in motorcarriage.

I halt on brim of granite,
My eyes glance off the planet.
I begin to slice the blood orange,
It leaks streams of garnet.

I want to teach you something
about life ephemeral.
Eyes like ruby,
Mind like emerald.

A Split Shake

Who knows what the future holds?
Who knew life without you could be so cold?
Who can tell how our fortune unfolds?

The natural passage is to resolution.
Watch it fall according to my profusion,
Watch the future manifest,
One moment in resplendence.

Our eyes feast the brilliance,
The gravity begins to impress.

Drawn down into canals of despair,
Or riding the bright rainbow's glare,
Every moment should be shared.

Love should catch you unaware,
and drag you out of the past
with its white smile flared.

Sweeping Webs

Rats in the cheddar,
Bogeys under the couch.
I'm etching this letter
as I wish to kiss
that creamy pout.

Fish in your percolator,
Worms in the lettuce.
Widows in your computer,
Bats on the brim of the terrace.

Snakes in the kettle,
Hornets in every drawer.
I can never settle
Till I hold you evermore.

Now lizards on the terrace,
Frogs in the furnace.
My heart starts to perish
When you turn and vanish.

Crows in the cold,
Wasp on the wrist.
Is this fool's gold,
Or my rightful bliss?

Shadows in the shutters,
Blight-filled bookshelves.
Can you truly love another,
And still be yourself?

Apes on the paintings,
Owls fly out the cupboard.
I am nearly fainting,
Whenever we are severed.

Generation $

Let me tell you about
my generation—
We don't judge,
We don't hold a grudge,
And we never bloody budge.

We swim through seas
Of electric fudge,
We look for love lustrous
as the Sun.

We burn the green of avarice,
and lust forth, adventurous.

We love to shake, and vape,
and take shots.
We love to sear the mold
and slash the rot.

We love to remind you
of what you've forgot.

We'd like to rewind our digital clock.
We'd like to chill a minute,
And check our stock.
We'd like a gold lager
to flow into our bock.

I'll take a cold carbonado,
Dark as the galaxy.
Carved by an ancient maestro,

It fits you alluringly.

I'm checking into the master
under a false identity.
Violet velvet and alabaster,
Luxury is a serpentine entity.

Reign & Bow

Is this the life we're on now,
Is this the creature
My soul disavows?

Is this another day on the scales?
Between light and evil,
In clear streams
And black veils.

Is this another day
On nothing but
Bread so pale?

Say why you sail,
Say with hat in hand
Over the bulwark rail,
That you love our tale,
That your love never sways.

Whisper into my ear
of future quakes,
Let my fears
jade away.

Arrows

I'm losing a lot of blood,
river of rubies.
I'm turning back into mud,
Like something out of the movies.

Which of my seventy identities
Will rush forth from the ink?
Which of my caricatures
Will pull you back from the brink?

Which of my words
Are whetstone to your sword?
Which of my poems
Sensed your world?

A poem is a dragon
In golden flames whirled.

Davy Jones' Locker

Through the mirror
and into the darkest room.

Beyond the quivering
ocean blooms,

Over my heart in
impenetrable gloom,

I seal my soul
in a sunken tomb.

I buried my gold
On an isle blue,

Grip the wheel and wonder
If I can sail back to you.

Heads of the Hydrangea

When the night is a cold shiver,
When your sin has stolen your quiver,
When you can't even drown in liquor,
A knotted hand turns worms to wyverns.

The dawn lies undelivered,
My soul at the bed of the river,
My only hope a slipping sliver,
My sacred home simmering cindered.

The Crickets

It matters not how pretty you are,
Someday we both will fly.

It matters not how wealthy he is,
Our time is running dry.

I would never guess
As I held you on that
Old teak bridge,
That matters would flow to this.

I never wanted my spirit
To turn harsh as lye,

I never could bear
When the apple fell
From my eye.

My clock strikes nigh
And I am not fain to try.

A lock of hair,
A century's hibernation.
Does this give face
To our debasement?

Does our luck deserve
Its true placement?

Will we crawl,
Will we stride

From basement to balcony?

What will formulate
From the natural alchemy?

When will true evil
Be barred in penitentiary?

Beyond the hills,
Beyond the vales,
Past desiderata in gale,

When will a warm toast
Ring forth from chilling misery?

Trace of Path

If I have to die
let it be from laughter.
If I must bleed,
make it sangria out a pitcher.

If I must go blind,
Let it be in dazzling beauty.
If I hit the pit,
Let my breath taste fruity.

If I have gone mute
It should be to your concern.
If I cannot salute,
Thunderstruck taciturn,
I'll unthread what I yearn.

If I must take a lift,
Let it be this world from ash.
If I must love
In this searing gash,
Make it true, make it real, make it last.

Act II
Bountiful Circumstances

Lens & Form

I need darkness,
I need bright.
I crave wintry moon
And flickering candlelight.

I see oceans,
I see groves.
I see orchards painted in sunlight.

I breathe stars,
I sigh music.
I rewrite laws of physic.

I take a dream you witnessed,
And knock it off the chopping block.

I spread an unspoilt canvas,
And split it with a guillotine.

My future is brining
In cask on lien.
My life is of nature,
Yet at mercy to its means.

With darkness comes confusion,
Rattling brinks obscene.

At dawn, a glimpse
Of what was left to green.

I'm Going Somewhere

Never been before.
I'm breathing in aura
Of forgotten lore.

The night beseeches,
Before it implores.
To right are the peaches
Of your tender years.

Screeching aflight
are the peafowl in my tears.

The world may be yearning,
and sinking in fear,
Yet somehow each day
unravels into the clear.

Mourning Tides

Par the course,
with no remorse.

I like the way
The wind whistles
through the eaves.

Been awhile since I heard the dirge,
Twice a minute on wings of word.
Been a year of turning leaves,
Time spirals like golden wreaths.

Forge a path
Through winter's purge.
Step through the glass
of your darkest urge.

Lay on the pedal,
If you please.
Glide out of this metal
with fluid ease.

The wind is growling
through the breeze.
The night is howling
for some company.

The Wise Man

You can't write without a pen,
You can't roll without paper.
You can't tan without the sun,
You can't crunch without a wafer.

Try breathing with no air,
Try a drink with no water.
Try living a place where
the net is of fodder.

In the roaming glare,
At the brink of the coffer,
You turn from the blazing tear,
and inspect a Faustian offer.

Breaching Walls

The crown is aglow
with the pulse of rot.
This world's fortunes turn
like arrows on the watch.

The sages say two centuries
left in play.
But then this would all
be for naught.

The hordes advance on my mossy wall,
My hounds come out to call.
Terror breaks in my footfall,
Then rays of sunlight, green as emerald.

Unscrupulously Scrumptious

A beauty multifarious,
An embrace splendiferous.
Pulling aside lattice,
Stepping through trellis.

They will forget us,
After a tip of birettas.
Leaving behind what dreads us,
We will sew up this husk,
Before it resents us.

We will clear up this musk,
That stuns and upsets us.

We must be brusque
when love is upon us,
and ooze scarlet auras
like cherries crushed.

March of the Plume

You begin to rush,
and mush your steed
Down Violin Street.

Bar the peak,
Guard the deeds,
Sawfalls is under siege!

O'Sparrow's at the helm,
Tom is in the lead,
Of the Indigo Army and the Sapphire Seas.

There are fires in the elms,
And arrows in the eaves.
Time has come to turn this host of misery!

All isles ought join with others,
All men should shake like brothers.
No blood shall spill in these gutters.

No evil can live in these walls,
Our fortune outshines them all.
To arms for sweet Sawfalls!

The Social Chameleon

In solitude and solace
With a little latitude and no promise,
I slither out of the trellis
and into pergola most fine.

There I swam,
Hanging into the plaza,
Firm as pasta
before boiling time.

Clutching close the high wire,
Tail on the vine dire,
Tongue down into the mire,
Breaking free of the briar,
and into the bowers with adapting desire.

The End of Autumn

I remember the cold,
I remember the ire.
I live in a dream, a fleeting scene
of ice sculpture in hellfire.

I walk a plank between
Limestone and cloud-spire,
I can't conceive the prospect
to which you conspire.

I can't seem to redirect
my eye from this pyre,
But you must never slacken,
As the One, you shall never tire.

No, you will press on,
Through limestone to cloud-spire.

Nature of Man

Where the stone meets the soil,
Where the pools start to boil,
I tally my gold and check my oil.

Where the mines meet the toil,
When your plots come up foiled,
I sally from the gorge of midnight roil.

Let's take a trip down South,
Where the river meets the mouth,
Where volcanoes meet our route.

Let's go to golden hours,
When sweet comes of sour,
And towers are eaten by flowers.

Another Poem

Hmm… They call me the professor
in this nice patch of sky.

Huh… The teak of your dresser
is stained with rye.

Uhh… How to confess
your life is a lie?

Ohh… I won't stress when light
flickers and dies.

Ahh… To lay against your breast,
and all this implies.

Hah! The tears of your quest
have turned to butterflies.

Echoing Steps
For those close to me

I will not arrive at your door
in a black limousine.

I will not hit the landing strip
in a jet of silvery sheen.

I will not set sail for your port,
in a yacht on seas of green.

Perhaps step on wet flagstones,
Through the misty dark of dreams.

Perhaps a late-afternoon stroll,
Under canopy of sunbeams.

Perhaps a walk into our future,
Through puddles of distant memories.

Tomorrow we plummet on magic carpet
Through the arches of hematite.

Tomorrow we soar under balloons galore,
In skies amethyst and bright.

Tomorrow I'll grow wings of snow,
And we'll flutter off into the night.

Hidden Miracles

You don't need the book,
When you have the poet.
So dust that rust,
Then return it.

Listen to my verbs
as I speak them through a screen.
Drink my worlds,
Sip them like tea.

Something is burning
the fringe of this dream.
Our fortunes are turning like leaves off-green.
With this searing ruby, we defy winter's gleam.

With unshaken faith,
With convictions of iron,
With doubt on the pyre
beside false desire.

Slip into canals of cooling ire,
Waxen lies melt in true fire.
Blinking eyes at brilliant designs,
One is wont to deprive,
Ere he satisfies.

Fortunate Fire

For Jessica Lucarelli

Blessed is the love
That shines through me today.
I rise from a thousand-year sleep
To hear what your heart has to say.

This pulses much deeper
than any cavernous quay.
Today's muse is made
of different stock than yester-ways.

When she is near, eyes like emerald,
I burst passionate rays marigold.
My soul stretches out for her locks,
Like falls of molasses down pearly rock.

My heart cracks out of its amber,
I leave soft timbers as time loudly stops.
The days before you were steep, slow drops,
And every moment since, you shepherd my flock.

Broken Wonders

I am running out of miracles,
My font of youth has dried.
Empty are my cure-all phials,
My mirror of truth just lied.

My scrying bones gnawed clean,
My wishing well sprung a leak.
My guardian angel is green,
My gypsy grandmother won't speak.

My tarot are torn and tattered,
The Ouija is burned and battered.
My genie's off to Senegal,
With my crystal ball.

Shooting stars wink their backs at me,
The planets hide in gaseous obscurity.
That séance was soon to unwind,
My palms forever unlined.

My dreams are thorny as the rose,
My spread sea begins to close.
I suppose I will have to use my head,
And see clear signs of the Lord instead.

A Little Curiosity

It's secret poetry,
Only unlocked by this one key.
Life on the stone for all to see.

It's secret air,
For a chosen fellow to breathe.
Shell of tortoise in infinite sea.

It's a secret vision,
In spectra only some can see.
A love like solid ivory.

It's a secret song,
That plays on in a hidden key,
Echoing over whirling sea.

It's a secret draught,
In the caps of willowy reed,
That awakens your eye to See.

It's a secret scroll,
Locked in the bowers of eve.
But someone has left the key.

Frost So Fine

I was in a pretty dark place,
But you must stumble before you pace.

It's too much grief
to say goodbye.

It's too much trouble
to ask you why,
You are rainbows out of crimson quakes.

If I can have one favor,
Before I lie,
It is to kiss your golden grace,
And stare into those diamond eyes.

The Silken Sleigh
For Jessica Lucarelli

The stockings are all sewn,
The baubles hang with glee.
The hearth is glowing roan
With the spirit of your company.

The pie is sliced and warm,
The lights wink in the trees.
Tonight love is reborn
In glittering fantasy.

The way is shoveled bare,
Ice falls from the eaves.
Heaven is the earth where
The angel treads with me.

Your delight is my own,
Your pleasure, my legacy.
I am but melting snow
In the meadow of your purity.

Arriving in Miami

There are a dozen species on my deck,
A thousand clouds over this shipwreck.

There are a hundred causes
To soar like an eagle,
Spreading wings like axes
Of toffee-brown treacle.

There are a million days left
To take up the olive twig.
We cannot live bereft
Of sparkling stream and leafy sprig.

There are a ton of spices on my rack,
And infinite hours to seek what I lack.

Castle & Coach

There is a man's motor,
There you have his castle.
They did not grow like clover,
They are built of hustle and hassle.

To drink in those sapphires,
To tease those golden tassels,
I am gilt in tinseled bright desire,
Fit of your vassal, host and empire.

The race is done,
The jig mixed-up,
Steeds cease to gallop.

You may rest in man's triumph,
But without a heavenly mate
It will darken and deflate.

The Diamonds You Deserve

There is an eye that sees truth, not light.
There is sight only of candlelit night.

Is the dark growing clearer?
Can I dive a little deeper?
Will dusky glades ever burn bright?

Are we wandering soul,
Or pillar of gold?
Are we on shores of sky,
In waves of emerald?

Do we lounge on clouds of silver,
And sink into horizons scarlet?
Do we wade in azure river,
Is our passion bold as garnet?

Are my eyes blazing ruby,
Is your heart a cool sapphire?
Can I turn the night into a diamond,
So you will douse my fire?

Is there a love like obsidian?
An endless unspoken abyss,
Bottomless twists of morta,
Living millennia in the mist.

Tomorrow rises in fuchsia pearls,
Veins of topaz glimmer in your curls.
With a look of smelting tigerseye,
A crystal touch, and I am pulverized.

Sunken Coals

In the right canal,
To blue reef of coral.
On the true path,
On a way immortal—

Tradewinds guide my sloop
Through glowing portal.
Fortunes sing bell-clear
On white wings of order.

Our fears are being cooked in the corner.
Tell me what it means to be a mortal,
Tell me how it feels to be fired from a mortar.

How did a glacier
take down the Titanic?
Show me how David
slew mighty Goliath.

Explain how the world
Turns on its axis,
Count what has truly come of our taxes.

Earth is cleft by the edge of our axes.
One man fasts,
While another collapses.

An Unraveling

Maybe someday you will become
Something that you aren't now.
Perhaps entwining fates
Will take a proud bow.

These shadows won't crush me in their charms.
Forever isn't enough time to have you in my arms.

This morn won't wake me,
Not with all its alarms.

This night will forsake me,
When you are not in the stars.

This prison won't hold me,
Not with diamond bars.

While you tick on in deep freeze,
My heart erupts and chars.

Nighty Night

People may have made me great,
But the One turns me my best.
There's no such thing as frozen fate,
Put your cares to rest.

This, the winding track to my demise,
Flickers between men and butterflies.
Forget-me-nots adorn her shoulders,
The dewy earth eats our spurs.

Sweet rain floods away cries,
Truth twinkles in our words.
Is there justice in our world?
Will there be beef in the curd?

What makes your mind swirl?
What is the most pleasant verb?

How do You streak night and day
On the canvas of the Milky Way?

Sometimes a heart can survive alone,
And find all its ticks a squandered loan.

I Fade

I

I do not run from the truth,
I embrace it.
No two worlds are alike,
'Round the bend we must face this.

Yet we turn to our brothers in strife,
And they mirror us in kind.

Let these words settle
Into the droves of your mind.

Let unfurl steam from kettle,
Pray uncloud mist from eye.

See whirling bodies,
See crying time
Whisk with feathers
The diamond bedside.

You can sever me from forever,
If my path never leaves this bosk of blight.

Suppose you can slay me,
I am a creature of the night.

II

I do not run from my youth,

It was blue and full of grassy places.

The greens winked with a certain dew,
All was gleaming and thoroughbred.

There was a vigor in the trees,
Trumpets sounded in swarming bees.
Nature played a pure symphony.

There was this one day so azure,
It brought me to my knee.

The Sun beamed his love unto me,
The One set everything into being.

There were no clouds of doubt,
There was no rain in the vaults above.
It was a taste of life,
This hailstorm of love.

Act III
The Tale of King Thrushbeard

The Tale of King Thrushbeard

A lyrical drama in one act. A reimagining of a beloved Grimm fairy tale.

Dramatis Personae

The Maid Myrra—heiress apparent of Roote, rather hollow-hearted and exquisitely pulchritudinous.

King Roote—Myrra's father, lord of the land of Roote, a gallant courtier who is oft forthright to mask his ambivalence.

Julio—court jester, in service to King Roote, a shifty fellow with a shadowed countenance.

King Thrushbeard—lord of the land of Capresha, a courtier-knight in the vigor and folly of youth.

Orpus—a destitute lyrist, learned in the art of music.

Courtesans of the Maid *(five in number)*

King's Guard *(four men in service to King Roote)*

Pub Folk *(among them the Courtesans returning in humbler garb, and one barmaid)*

Queen Roote

Setting

The fantastical kingdoms of Roote and Capresha, in particular: a palace chamber, a palace garden, a wooded path, a cabin, a pub and a crown hall.

Scene I—Vanity of Vanities

Palace chamber. Myrra and Roote lounge in luxury. Julio strikes a slow, mournful tune on piano.

Myr.
Oh Father, I wish you'd find me a proper mate,
You've brought nothing but fools of late.
I fear I am to have a lonely death!
Why can't you bring me a lover worth a breath?

Roo.
I grieve, my sweet blue jay,
For I cannot find one to take you away.
Would that a fair knight would knock,
And you would be off with his noble stock.

Jul.
What is the matter,
Why do you gripe?
You are lords of this land,
Your time is ripe.

Myr.
Ah, but it troubles me so,
How the hours come and go.
Is there nothing that can be done,
To find a noble, pure one?

Roo.
Such is the state we bind and grate,
Such is our miserable fate.
Aye! Bring forth another brigade,

Perhaps our woe may yet degrade.

Enter five Courtesans and Thrushbeard in the rear. They line up and salute Roote. Myrra drearily inspects each of them in turn.

Myr.
No, no, Father this won't do at all,
This one is much too small.
And round as a kettle,
With those veins, too.
Must be quick to nettle,
And fond of brew.

And this knight, tall as a fountain,
Looks brittle as dust of the mountain.
Go your merry way, you reed, you stalk of beans,
And torment me no more with your measly means.

No, no, Father this won't do at all,
This one has no gall.
He is weathered like the chicken coop,
His time long roosted away.
What I could say of those strands of gray,
Would surely turn him to goop.

And this chap, though spry and limber,
Looks too much a turncoat for my taste.
In battle he would fall like timber,
And so is unfit to guard this glorious face.

No, no, Father this won't do at all.
This one must be the curtain call.

A mere child sets the scene,
A lad of perhaps fourteen.
How is a boy to arrange
For whom this kingdom sparsely retains?

My stars, good heavens! It couldn't be,
A man with a chin like the branch of a tree.
You are strange, good sir, completely weird,
I hereby dub thee Thrushbeard!

   She points to the door. Exeunt Courtesans, in
gloomy gait.

I'm taking my carriage to some canyon or crag,
Likely throw myself off.
If this is the best you have.

Roo.
Offspring, you are too choosy, too vain, too prim,
Nothing delights you, your future is grim.
I have failed as your Father, I have failed as a man,
One can only hope for signs of divine plan.

Jul.
(In aside to Roote) Send out the girl,
You and I ought to have a word.

Roo.
Myrra, leave us, I must take council,
With this fool, this minstrel, this scoundrel.

   Exit Myrra in a huff.

Jul.
Now that we are quite alone,
I can say you must never condone
The sparing and spoiling of a child as yourn—
Her fate is written like the lining of a storm.

Roo.
What can be done? I know you've an answer,
Tell me this minute, or I'll throw you to the panthers!

Jul.
It is simple, sire, clear as a drum,
But I fear thereafter you'll fall and crumb.
I am to tear you in twain,
With these tidings of pain.

Roo.
On with it, lad,
Before I go mad.

Jul.
You had best send out the girl,
To fare the cruel world.
Yes, you had best send out the girl,
To fare the cruel world.

Curtain.

Scene II—Ascent of the Lyrist

Palace garden. Front gate is visible. Myrra sits at a marble vanity, primping in a large mirror. Lush botanicals adorn the scene. A light tweeting of birds accents the words of Myrra.

Myr.
Ah, we cling to the days,
Though we know their ways
To be painful and untrue.
Yet we cling to them like glue.

Oh, we hold the dream
We were meant to be,
Though it falters, tearfully,
As we flicker into dreams of history.

Yes, we chain ourselves to a moment,
In the midst of life's portents and potions.
We love each and every movement,
But then that moment is a drop in the ocean.

Aye, we fill the present,
Turn it into skin, cloth and resin.
Yet something's amiss when one ticks alone,
A filly's nothing if she isn't roan.

Enter Roote, Julio, King's Guard.

What is it, Father, can't you see
I'm trying to spin poetry?
And you, ghast-armored mongers,

Paint a portrait, it shall last longer.

Roo.
Stand back, my men, and let me speak,
I must these words, though my heart does wreak.

(Aside to Myrra) Daughter, the time has come,
For you to fare the rabbit's run.
The next man who knocks at the gate,
Will take you away to Lord-knows what fate.
I will cast you out with the clothes on your back,
Not a farthing of silver in your sack.

Myr.
You must be jesting,
If you are truly suggesting
That any old ram will do.
Come, Father, you know it is untrue.
And how am I to survive winter's sting,
Without my royal retinue?
The icy clifts and snowy sheen
Will pick my bones clean.

What am I to do in the spring,
Lay out on the dew like a common thing?
It is unfit for one of my status,
To steep below the cloudy stratus.

And how shall I soak the summer,
Drenched with rain, damp as a cellar?
Begging for a rag, a greasy tatter,
To cover my head in the hot splatter.

And then what about autumn,
Will I shrivel like a leaf so glum?
Shall I cleave the wood, toil and hammer,
As each of my charms snuffs out like a glamer?

Roo.
Sweet daughter, you plead in vain,
The verdict is sewn, my heart is in twain.
I am sending you out, I will not refrain.
You shall fare the world, may it spare you pain.

*Myrra swoons. He rushes over to steady her.
A moment later, the knocker of the gate is struck. A
Guard spreads the doors. Enter Orpus, bowing in
servility.*

Orp.
Good day, merry gentlemen,
I wonder if you might spare a hen?
Or perhaps, if there is work to be done,
I strum a mean lyre, know my way 'round a pun.

Jul.
Aye, we'll work you like a pony,
You're to take this maid in sweet matrimony.
I'm sure you'll make her a fine mare,
Target of many a jealous stare.

Roo.
Curse this day,
Silence, you swine!
You had better pray
This does not unwind.

Myrra comes to in her Father's arms.

Myr.
(Faintly) Where am I? Am I home?
How much time has flown?

Roo.
The jig, dear daughter, is up I'm afraid,
Your grass is grown.
You're with him now, I won't be swayed.
You're on your own.

Myr.
Ha! Such is the thought,
I already have, like it or not.
I expected you to turn your back to me,
Your heart gleams so icily
Before the standards of my beauty.

Is this him? Is this the desperate fool,
With whom I'm to walk this tightrope cruel?
So be it, I care not anymore,
My own father has cast me on death's door.

And you, my little jester,
I know your hand in this.
I promise that you'll fester,
Until you and my dagger sweetly tryst.

Roote is breaking. He looks regretful, but afraid of standing down in front of the Guard.

Roo.
I declare you married before the Lord.
Now be off before I draw my sword!
So it is, the gravel with you,
Before I shed tears bright and blue.

Roote collapses on the bench.

Orp.
It is not so grim, my maid, my mare,
Love is never a crystal stair.
Come, we are off on our merry way,
Sunbeams shine, we must seize day.

Exeunt Myrra and Orpus out the gate, the former in great displeasure, the latter humming for his good fortune. The Guard fills the gate to prevent reentry.

Roo.
Oh, Julio, what have you done?
I am the greatest fool under the sun,
For trusting in your devices,
You see my heart, how it ices.
My only issue faring the cold world,
Not even a shawl on the precious girl!

Jul.
Sir, it will be for the best,
Though it seems a tempest.
We'll guard from afar,
Track what transpires.
We'll stick to the briar,

And not light a fire.

Roo.
Thanks to you, I'll be a beggar in the bush,
Lord of the vines like some king of Cush.
Men, gather me my gear,
I'm camping tonight, can't you hear?

Curtain.

Scene III—Steps of Sorrow

Orpus leads Myrra through a wood to his cabin, its facade present to the far right. A town and a coliseum are painted in the distance. Orpus gently strums his lyre.

Orp.
Tell me, dove, if your soul can bear,
What do you think of this forest so fair?

Myr.
Who reigns over this wood so great?

Orp.
It belongs to King Thrushbeard,
Would be yours, were you his mate.

Myr.
Oh, why did I call him wick and weird,
Curse my stars, damn my fate!
My hexes burn like a grill,
My tongue upon a hot anvil.

Orp.
Come now, it's not so dark,
You have me, my lovely lark.

Myr.
And who rules over this town so bright?

Orp.
It is under King Thrushbeard,

At noon and at night.

Myr.
Oh, why did I call him wick and weird,
Curse my stars, damn my blight!
The words sear like a white poker,
Cackled back by that horrid joker.

Orp.
Come now, you'll not wander twilight,
You have me to keep keel upright.

Myr.
Who reigns over this arena so vast?

Orp.
Grounds of King Thrushbeard,
My dear old lass.

Myr.
Oh, why did I call him wick and weird,
Curse my stars, blast the past!
I feel blown through the bellows,
Straight into flaming throes.

Orp.
Come now, let's see a smile,
We're getting on meanwhile.

Myr.
And who is captain
Of this ship so grim?

Orp.
That would be yours truly,
And you'll not find it so ghouly,
So ghastly and unruly,
If you work the charms within.
In fact, you'll see it quite cooly,
Once I carry you 'cross the brim.

Myr.
Not so fast, sonny Jim,
I don't love you, 'tis not my whim.
There is no chance in heaven,
That you will carry me 'cross that brim.

Orp.
Very well, but you won't step it otherwise,
Enjoy your sojourn, Lady of the Flies.

Myr.
Hmph, would that it be,
Rather than accept that indignity.

     Exit Orpus through the cabin door. Myrra takes repose on a stump in despair. Enter Roote and Julio, creeping in the brush.

Roo.
(Aside to Julio) There she is, you bloody knave!
Not a pip, or your head on my glaive!

     Roote twitches, frustrated, as he examines his progeny's predicament. He tries to hold his peace, but he cannot help but speak after a moment.

There she blows, so sad and distraught,
The very fruit these loins have wrought.
My frozen heart is caught,
Snaring my every thought.

Ought I end this black charade,
And sweep her to the palisade,
So she may lounge on the willowy loam?
I fear for her dear, dulcet life,
When she is without our hospitable home,
Her shadow bruises like a butter-knife.

Jul.
Aye, sir, but it must wait,
Think she's gaining a humbler gait.

Myr.
Good heavens, I am not alone!
Run thither, you coward, you crow!
Do me no harm, I am of royal blood,
Heaven's hand holds my maidenhood.

Roo.
Curse you, you heathen, you hellion,
You shattered our shield, dratted rapscallion!
Tie up your tunic, run like a gust,
With any luck, all is not bust.

Exeunt Roote and Julio in haste.

Myr.
Oh, why do the stars curse me so,

Was I not a sweet, dainty doe?
Out here in the peals of heat,
Lusting for my chamber neat.

I miss the holly hill of home,
The blue birds, the green loam.
Why must I fare this pit of despair?
My spirit is shattered beyond repair!

I suppose I'm doomed to sink,
This wood has me on the brink.
Heaven forgive my weakening will!
I must knock on the beggar's sill.

     *Myrra knocks on the window. Orpus' head
appears in the threshold.*

Orp.
Well, my dapper dear,
Have you lost the fear?
Are you of the sensation
To love without moderation?

Myr.
Orpus, I am ready to love,
But with the coolness of a dove.

Orp.
Very well, come in my arms,
Let me show you the mean of charms.

     *Exeunt Orpus and Myrra, the one carrying the
other over the threshold into the cabin. Curtain.*

Scene IV—Havoc of the Honeymoon

Interior of Orpus' humble cabin. The two sit on harsh stone furnishings. Orpus strums the lyre, attempting to drown out Myrra's disparaging statements.

Myr.
This is no home, a hovel at best,
There're bees in the bonnet and rats in the crest.
You cannot seriously expect
A maid like me to sail this shipwreck.

What will come next, clouds of dreck?
Shall I sweep the attic's hornet nest?
I think I will take the blustery wind,
Than be in a house where spiders spin.

Orp.
There is no shackle on your shin,
You are here on your whim.
Perhaps be loving of what life affords,
Maybe sit back and soak in my chords.

Myr.
Be loving of what life affords?
Surely you jest, my dreary lord.
Contrariwise you are untoward,
To strum so over my retorts.

Orp.
Music waits for no man,
Just like sandglass sand.

You make the food of love
Sound like grinding bran.

Myr.
Is this the harmony
Of sweet matrimony?
We have but stepped in,
And discord drops to din.

Orp.
An answer to make your skin quiver—
You will see the toxin in the mirror.

Myr.
And you're a fresh phial of panacea,
Cruel kidnapper king of nausea.
Want to act on what I desire?
Take me back to my lofty spire.

Orp.
You know that will not do,
Your own father will not have you.
Perhaps stem the poison from your maw,
And dull your claws like the bandsaw.

Myr.
Pernicious lips and dagger nails,
This, my soul behind the veils?
You know not the perils and travails
Of possessing beauty that impales.

One must repel the many glares,
The innumerous envious stares.

One must have a carapace of steel
To endure the spur of the public heel.

Orp.
Such is your sorrowful life, I suppose?
You've no clue what the unsightly oppose.
They are speared as they step the brim
Of the pearly halls you waltz so prim.

Myr.
Their lot, not mine—
Life for a maid must be fine.
It is the will of the world
To be in the palm of this girl.

Orp.
It is the will of this jungle,
For you to toil for your fill.
Now, make this tambourine ring,
In time to the melody of my strings.

*The tune increases in pitch, Orpus gets up and begins
to hop around. He pulls Myrra out of her seat. Myrra
begrudgingly begins to smack the instrument.*

Dance, sweet maid, dance,
Swing your hips in a trance.
You'll make them laugh, make them clap,
Make the silver flow out of my cap.

You'll make me proud,
Work your sire woe,
That he allowed

The exile of his doe.

Let your legs fall to trance,
That's it, darling, dance!
You're clutched by the root,
You've nothing but your suit.

You shall work like the peasants,
The servants of your house.
You shall have your presence
Shrunken down to a mouse.

Myr.
May I speak, dear Orpus?
The pink snake writhes.
There is no need to bore us,
I am paying my tithes.

Curtain.

Scene V—The Brittle Maid

> *Interior of a rugged tavern, The Nightingale.*
> *Myrra and Orpus tune their instruments on a small*
> *stage to one side. Men sit about despondently, catered*
> *to by a single overworked barmaid. Roote and Julio*
> *are huddled in the corner opposite the couple. They*
> *are hooded but recognizable.*

Orp.
Are you ready to play,
To shake and sashay?
Ready to take on
The bard's baton?

Myr.
Oh, the dread is peaking,
The fear is wreaking.
The hot air leaking,
My misery creaking.

Orp.
That's the spirit,
You black old beast.
You don't know to fear it,
You don't the least.

Be a humble lass,
Or you'll sleep on the grass.
Soften your presence,
Or you'll fly with the pheasants.

Myr.
Aye, body wills, yet soul fails,
Why am I cast in treacherous travail?
A butterfly on tacks,
A star in a spyglass.

Woe! This beauty
Does not hark
For a common body,
A vulgar lark.

How can I pretend to the graces,
Of a wench with a thousand faces?
With their eyes' eating traces,
My heart turns and races.

Do you enjoy debasement and harassment?
Do you thrive on unpleasantness?
I would rather be cast on the pavement,
That live in your yoke, your clutch, your harness.

Oh, though you coat my heart in black varnish,
My golden aura will never rust and tarnish.
I will fly free of your binding chain,
And restore the crystal of my name.

Orp.
Shake off your shame,
Slip whim of your bane.
Shimmy without your brain,
Slide like it's pouring rain.

Yeah, break off the blame,

Let the guilt melt away.
You shall play this game,
Free of irons of yesterday.

Yes, shake off your shame,
You're wild, not a lick tame.
Forget your proper manners,
Boast your charms with banners!

*Orpus begins a jaunty tune. Myrra dances
reluctantly. The pub-folk stand and gather before the
stage.*

Roo.
(In aside to Julio) What's this the bloody knave's on?
Having my dear dance like a pawn!
I'll gut him like some slimy prawn,
And save my bejeweled faun.

Jul.
(In aside to Roote) No, no, he's putting on air,
To tame that dame so fair.
He's bubbling up her spirit,
No matter how you near it.

1st Man.
Aye, there she is, ruby of the squall,
The sad strumpet who said I'm too small.
And now you shall kiss my shoes,
Bow to the credit on your dues.

Orp.
On the ground, my gal,

A penny please, my pal.

Roo.
(More audibly now) Woe! So damn dreadful,
So bitter and painful.
I'll take the rusty guillotine
Over a moment of this scene.

2nd Man.
There she is, the maid so vile,
Who said I was frail and fragile.
And now you shall sew my shirt,
You know the body is but dust and dirt?

Orp.
To his hems, my dear,
A coin in the cap here.

Jul.
(Still in aside to Roote) See something noble at hand,
There's a skill you never planned.

3rd Man.
There she stands, I feel so cold,
The cruel mistress who called me old!
You're working now, bought and sold,
Come hither and bite these crowns of gold.

Orp.
Let's see that smile, sweet lass,
Go on then, give the cap a pass.

Roo.

Nay! Her glass jaw will give way,
Will break like dew in light of day!

4th Man.
Hm, so it seems, in suitable stance,
She who took saintly patience
For spineless diffidence.
For a shred of silver, you shall prance.

Orp.
Aye, give him your graces,
Let's see those royal faces.

5th Man.
Oh, there blows the brutal blight,
Who hailed me spry and sprite.
Know that youth has fire in his eyes,
And many miles before he dies.

Orp.
Toss him the cap,
Toss it in my chap!

Myr.
My, my,
My soul shall cry.
Wingless, beaten,
Sinking in lye.

My, my,
My spirit will die.
Lain to rest

In the streams of my eyes.

Curtain.

Scene VI—Blooms

Crown hall, Kingdom of Capresha. Myrra is led in by Orpus.

Orp.
Here, my dear maid,
Now that you've finished at the loom,
Take up yon broom
And raid the dust of this room.

Myr.
But Orpus, I tire, I weather, I bawl,
You whip me after a moment's stall.
I need some peace, a nap at least,
If I am to clean at all.

Orp.
Nonsense! Balderdash!
You'll scour the cache and wipe the ash.
You will rinse the glass
And buff the brass.

I'm off for a pint,
And if you don't pull your weight,
You will find mice on your plate.

Now my dear, my maid, my peer,
Make haste. There is little time to waste.

Exit Orpus.

Myr.
Curse that cur, pitiful and small.
If my father knew,
He would carry his pall.
Oh, I am so blue,
My spirit's in freefall.

I am so remiss,
But I must sweep this
Cloud, mites and all.
My curtain has really come to call.

I suppose I ought to begin,
Perhaps this will sweep away my sin.

Myrra begins to sweep.

Will I ever restore
My crown in the clouds?
Will I ever again adorn
My gowns, my tiara, my shrouds?

Will that wolf ever tire and relent?
Will I pass before my gold is spent?
Will dawn rise of dusky fen,
Will grass grow in snowy glen?

Can a maid survive these burning portents,
And awful rats that bicker and fence?
Oh, I should hold the future in sight,
My stars must be hot and bright.

Perhaps I will yet be rescued,

By a silver-armored knight.
Perhaps I will again be imbued
With the dawn of my heart's delight.

But what will come of me?
I feel a stomped honeybee.
And how will I manage
In this toil of a marriage?

*Enter Orpus as Thrushbeard, in his true
attire. He removes the beard disguising his distinctive
chin, much to Myrra's shock. Enter the Courtesans,
attending Thrushbeard. Enter King and Queen Roote
beaming brightly, the Guard attending them. Enter
Julio, his face dark.*

Thr.
Excellent, my dear,
Preparations are complete.
Set aside your fear,
For the occasion is sweet.

You see, I have been testing
Your heart and heather,
As I took the guise
Of Orpus the beggar.

I wanted to know if you would grow,
Even in the darkest shadow.

I wanted to see if you would relent,
When your heart cried in dissent.

I wanted to know your temper under pressure,
With scarce enough gold to measure.

I wanted to feel you by my side,
When you had nothing but your pride.

Roo.
Do not think I forgot you,
Through these trials of doom.
I dogged your every step,
I guarded your every breath.

Take this noble King Thrushbeard,
For your lord, your rock.
May our countries be cleared,
For the queen of the lot!

Que.
Oh, how you have grown,
How time has flown!
I escape my weary travels
To give you this gown of jewels.

You will shine like the Sun's glower,
You will glimmer like this pearly tower.
Now dress, and primp, and powder,
As befit the maid of the hour.

Myr.
Oh, I don't know what to say,
A miracle shines today!
A rainbow paves the way,
My heart is songbirds in the bay.

Exit Myrra.

Jul.
So this is it,
Truth revealed.
We won't revisit
Her sudden zeal?

I still feel she will have my head,
Though her life has turned to gold from lead.
Come King, we ought counsel,
Over this sudden wedding tinsel.

Roo.
Silence, knave, have a little taste,
You will not cast doubt
On this day of golden grace.

Julio bows and steps back. Enter Myrra in her wedding gown, with a small gold crown.

Myr.
Well, the stage is set,
I have no regret.
Thrushbeard, I take you now,
Come, let us speak the vow.

Thr.
Yes, my dear, Myrra come here.
You will never again shed a tear.

You will rule this kingdom, this earth, this land.

In dreams you will be girt,
In the clouds you will stand.

In this fountain of worlds,
What is a king's command?

This country a barren waste,
If you do not take my hand.

Curtain.

www.ingramcontent.com/pod-product-compliance
Lightning Source LLC
Chambersburg PA
CBHW021131020426
42331CB00005B/718